# Self-Inflicted Overload

## Joyce E. Brooks

Forward by Chief Ivor J. Brooks
Illustrations by Brianna Bolden

Self-Inflicted Overload
*Five Steps to Achieving Work-Life Balance and Becoming Your Very Best*
Copyright © 2012
Joyce E. Brooks

Published 2012 by Rocky Heights Print & Binding
206 Oak Mountain Circle
Pelham, Alabama 35124

ISBN-13
978-1-937908-04-1

Forward by Chief Ivor J. Brooks
Illustrations by Brianna Bolden

# Dedication

*Jae and Matthew, I dedicate this book to you.*

*My greatest joy is being your Mommy.*

*You are my motivation to become my very best.*

*I love you with all my heart.*

# Contents

Foreword-------------------------------------------------------------7

Introduction--------------------------------------------------------9

Part I: KEEPING IT REAL

    Work-Life Balance-------------------------------------13

    My Only Responsibility-------------------------------19

    Got PEACE?-----------------------------------------------23

Part II: PEACE

    Step 1: Pray---------------------------------------------31

    Step 2: Energize---------------------------------------35

    Step 3: Adjust Your Attitude-------------------------39

    Step 4: Communicate---------------------------------43

    Step 5: Enjoy-------------------------------------------49

Part III: On Your Mark, Get Set, Choose-----------------------57

    Helpful Hints for Work-Life Balance----------------63

    Self-Inflicted Overload PEACE Contract-----------71

    Acknowledgements-------------------------------------73

    Biographical Sketch-----------------------------------75

# *Foreword*

Joyce E. Brooks asked me to read her manuscript entitled Self-Inflicted Overload and give her some feedback. Initially, I viewed the request as a kind gesture on her part to be inclusive. However, she made it very clear, she wasn't writing this book for self-promotion or a new hobby. She wanted to write a practical book that would help any person, regardless of gender, race, religious affiliation, marital status, or economic status, to achieve work-life balance and ultimately become their very best.

Joyce holds a B.S. and Master's degrees in electrical engineering. As an engineer, she understands the process of coming up with solutions to a problem. She approached the production of this book in the same manner. To ensure she produced the best piece of work, one solution would be to seek honest feedback and use that feedback to improve on the manuscript. Now that I had clear instructions on what was expected of me, I began the task of being a critic.

First, it was an easy read. It was not a lecture, but a conversation. Joyce starts off with what she sees as the ultimate perfected life. By the end, a practical perfected life emerges. The book lays out a plan of action to achieve work-life balance. Throughout the book, the reader is reminded of their role in self-inflicted overload. From personal experiences, trials, and errors, the author developed a plan that resulted in her limiting the overload and improving the quality of life for her and her family.

As she opens up about dealing with everything from being diagnosed with breast cancer to managing a family while pursuing a career, the reader is taken on a journey learning each of the five steps. Pray, energize, adjust your attitude, communicate, and enjoy are the steps of the strategy. Collectively, the strategy leads one to peace. Joyce achieved a state of being where there is tranquility and all things are in as close to equilibrium as humanly possible. This is what she offers to the reader.

As the husband of the author, I admit I had some preconceived ideas. Like, this book is written for women, and only women could relate to this book. I gained much more than I expected. I began the reading as a critic. By the end of the book, I found the advice valuable and considered ways to incorporate a few of the strategies to limit my load.

I am so proud of Joyce. She continues to amaze me. Not only is she a loving wife and mother, dedicated career woman, servant, community advocate, aspiring artist, playwright, and let me not forget, First Lady of the Fire Department. She has now managed to achieve work-life balance, minimized the overload, and then, written a book about it. Congratulations, Wife.

Ivor J. Brooks Sr., Fire Chief

Birmingham Fire and Rescue Service

# Introduction

Balancing all the responsibilities of work and life can be daunting, tiresome, and sometimes downright frustrating. How do I know this? I, too, found the responsibilities of work and life daunting, tiresome, and, on countless occasions, downright frustrating. I felt this way, because I attempted to be a superwoman without the super powers.

I tried to do everything for everybody, all the time, perfectly. And the moment I forgot to give my child lunch money, pick up dinner at a drive-through, or ran late for a meeting, I felt like a super failure. Where were my superwoman powers at these times? Nonexistent.

I can recall observing my mother's daily duties of cooking, cleaning, helping with homework, ironing, paying bills, caring for her children, grandchildren, and sometimes, the neighbor's children. There were probably many more duties associated with being a full-time, stay-at-home Mom raising seven children; I just wasn't aware of them.

The world I live in today is much different from the world my mother lived in. This does not mean she did not work as hard. I actually believe my mother's generation worked harder than my generation. My Mom did not have access to the resources that are available to us today. She did not manage banking online, enroll the children in after-school programs, or pick up dinner at a drive-through window. Today, we have access to all those things and much more.

My mother epitomized the superwoman. She appeared to have everything under control. Never did I hear her complain, nor did I see her shed a tear about her circumstances.

As I attempted to be a loving wife, a great mother, and an ambitious career woman, I found myself complaining and on occasion, crying. Yes, I cried. Why? I just could not manage to keep it all together. I was failing; and for me, failure was my greatest fear. Failure would have so many dreadful consequences...or so I thought.

What was I to do? As the saying goes, mother knows best. Off to my mother I went to ask her a couple of questions: "How did you do it? How did you handle all those responsibilities and not lose your mind?" Her response: "You just do what you have to do." Initially, her response seemed quite ambiguous. Over time, it has finally become clear.

Doing what you have to do is nothing more than having a strategy that is designed for your circumstances. What works for Mom may or may not work for me. What works for me may or may not work for you.

Everyone needs a strategy to achieve work-life balance.

I am like many women who wear many hats, have countless responsibilities, and have high expectations. This combination can be either a blessing or a curse, depending on your perspective. I choose to believe it is a blessing. I have finally accepted two key facts about keeping it all together:

**Perfection does not exist, and losing sleep does not change your circumstances.**

Accepting these facts, along with personal experience, challenges, and errors, led me to come up with a strategy to achieve work-life balance. I believed that if I had a plan, I could successfully minimize the overload, enjoy a better quality of life, and become my very best. That is my hope for you as well.

On the pages that follow, I offer you my strategy to help you on your journey—journey where peace becomes the norm and the daily responsibilities of life don't wear you down.

Welcome to PEACE—five steps to achieving work-life balance.

**Part I**

# Keeping It Real

"...I attempted to be a superwoman
without the super powers."

# Work-Life Balance

It is 5:30 a.m., and I hear the morning news as I complete the last 20 minutes of my hour-long workout. National headlines include the continuation of peace in the Middle East and the end of Third World poverty and famine. The Dow is up for the 27th consecutive day. The president signs into law, "Let's Go to School and Not Jail," which will provide adequate funding for public education. There was full support and no dissention in both the House and Senate, no morning traffic, and only a 10 percent chance of rain. Yes, a perfect day begins.

Just before I step into the shower, I check the scale. Great! I lost another pound. As I complete my shower, what do I hear? The men in my life—loving husband and two precious sons—are sitting at the kitchen counter eating a healthy breakfast, dressed, and ready to go to work and school. My arrival is greeted with kisses and compliments.

After a little pep talk to the big boy, off to work he goes. It is time to take the boys to school. Before heading out the door, I sign assignment pads and place snacks in their backpacks. Let's listen to a little praise on the satellite radio on the way to school. There is no need to referee with well-mannered, respectful children. The last words I hear before the boys exit the car: "Love you, Mommy."

Returning to the house, I take care of a few chores, return calls, confirm speaking engagements, and send a "love u" text to my husband. It is my day to volunteer to work with the tour ministry at 16th Street Baptist Church, so I fluff my hair, put on a little makeup, and off to church I go.

Two hours later and I'm in the produce section of my favorite grocery store buying fresh, non-chemically treated chicken for today's dinner. My cell phone rings. It's Mom and Dad. All is healthy, happy, and well at my parents' home.

Next, I am off to the carpool line to pick up the boys. No homework tonight. They completed their homework in class. Isn't it great to have children who love school and take the initiative to do their homework at school?

We are home, and I prepare dinner. I look out the kitchen window and enjoy watching the neighborhood kids and my sons shooting a little b-ball. My husband returns home to be greeted by a kiss after a long day at the office. It's 6 p.m., and we sit down and enjoy a gourmet dinner prepared by me. Oh, how I enjoy the dinnertime. It's the time we catch up, share stories, and laughter. What a great husband. He tells me not to worry about cleaning the kitchen and that he will take care of it.

I go upstairs and read bedtime stories with the boys. They have no interest in watching TV. They would rather read, listen to music, or build things with LEGOs. It is 8 p.m. The boys are tucked in tight. Lights out. Kiss. Kiss. "Good night, love you, sweet dreams, see you in the morning!"

My husband is finishing up in the kitchen, so I head to Studio J. Studio J is my laundry room/art room. I sit down to a blank canvas, and my creative juices just pour out. One hour later, I have completed another masterpiece. Painting is so liberating and relaxing. There are no rules or limitations.

Time to retire for the night. I hear Marvin Gaye serenading me—"Let's Get It On, Oh Baby." As I approach, I smell lavender candles burning. I think someone is waiting for dessert. I know what time it is. Do you? I am not going to share those details. This is not that kind of book. What a perfect end to a perfect day.

BUZZ! BUZZ! BUZZ! What? There goes the alarm clock; and then, I wake up. It was just a dream.

## *Reality*

The description of the perfect day is extremely satisfying. Everyone is happy, no stress, no drama, and ample time to do everything you want to achieve each day. What I described is not my reality. I would guess I am not the only person who has a vision of the perfect day but hasn't achieved it.

Not having work-life balance is a major stumbling block to achieving one's desires (i.e., the perfect day, quality relationships, a happy family, healthy living, peace, and the list goes on and on).

Work-life balance is achieved when the obligations that come with a career and the responsibilities of daily life are in equilibrium. Neither work nor life has a dominant role. In the correct balance, one will experience a state of tranquility, which translates to PEACE.

The opposite is also true. Too much work and too little living or too much living and too little work translates to problems, frustration, and, in my case, illnesses.

Let's accept that the perfect life does not exist. The next best thing would be a life that is not filled with problems, frustrations, illnesses, and uncertainty. Life will present the unexpected. You can bet on that. Reducing the number of these occurrences can be achieved by balancing work and life. Once balance exists, you have the confidence and strength to deal with whatever knocks at your door, including the unexpected.

Dividing time among numerous daily activities contributes to achieving work-life balance. Unfortunately, we often fail to balance the time between activities appropriately. You would think that out of 24 hours, one could find an hour to exercise, but squeezing one hour out of the day seems impossible when there are so many priorities.

**Activities that contribute to work-life balance when performed daily**

**TIP:**

o **Adequate sleep** – Ideally, eight hours each night

o **Balanced meals** – Breakfast, lunch, dinner, and healthy snacks

o **Organized home** – Ability to find items without extensive searching

o **Well-mannered children** – Less time disciplining leaves energy to expend elsewhere

o **Physical activity** - Work out for an hour a day

o **Healthy relationships** – Quality time with family, friends, spouse, and others

o **Meditation time** – Designated time to unwind; "Me" time

From first-hand experience, I've found that pursuing the American Dream—living in the future and self-inflicted overload – were all factors that made it very difficult to achieve work-life balance. I managed to overcome the idea of the American Dream and living in the future. However, it was self-inflicted overload that required much more focus and reasoning.

## *The American Dream*

Commercials and advertisements are one of many avenues of promoting the American Dream. Advertisers promote products by creating a picture of life that appears to be perfect, but this perfection seems to only occur when you drive the right car, weigh 110 pounds, and have perfectly behaving children and unlimited cash flow.

We often pursue the American Dream as defined by those who are focused on their bottom lines. I was guilty. I found myself working like crazy to obtain the resources to get big girl toys. I was always on a diet. In the end, I did not achieve perfection, nor did I lose any weight.

I believe the American Dream is the right and privilege of every United States citizen. However, it should not be a cookie-cutter design. The American Dream should be designed based on what is important to your bottom line. Today, I have a better understanding of what is really important to *my* bottom line. It is without a doubt family, faith, and PEACE. Focusing on these three things has led to the fulfillment of my American Dream.

## *Living in the Future*

Living in the future and not in the present is nothing more than an abuse of time. Each person is given 24 hours in each day. How you use those 24 hours is strictly up to you. Unfortunately, some people tend to spend today worrying about tomorrow. As a result, today is filled with lost opportunities.

Focusing on today has enabled me to do things that I could never have imagined. I can now profess that I am an artist; I have written and directed plays. I do not rush when sharing quality time with friends and family. I see things that were invisible before, because I was so dialed into tomorrow and not the "now."

I hope this does not shock you, but, tomorrow is not promised. We should learn to live in the present but plan for the future. Manage the future when it arrives.

Today should be the priority.

I haven't always valued today. In the pursuit of an engineering degree, I only focused on graduation, which was years down the road. Every semester I took classes that brought me closer to graduation. I had tunnel vision. I did not balance school and life back then. It wasn't until my senior year that I found out students could get into all the games free. Yes, I earned the degree, but I did not experience the adventures while achieving it.

## Self-Inflicted Overload

Self-inflicted overload is the third factor that contributes to a state of imbalance. This factor was the most challenging for me to overcome. It is also the reason I developed a strategy to achieve work-life balance. When you are overloaded, there is too much on your plate. There isn't enough time in the day to complete every task you feel you must complete. And you never say no, even when you know the request will push you over your limits.

Let's look at the facts: No one forces you to fill your plate. No one says you have to do everything today. The world will not come to an end if you do not finish everything on your to-do list, and no one makes you say yes when you know you should say no. This is self-inflicted overload.

The funny thing about self-inflicted overload is that it is usually followed by a state of denial. Imagine picking up a pistol and mistakenly shooting yourself in the leg. What do you do? First, you need to call for help, but no, you can't admit to anyone that you caused this hurt and pain. As you continue to bleed, you think of ways to cover up what has happened. In the meantime, the pain is getting worse. What was originally a bad situation has turned into a tragic situation. A tragedy caused by the denial of the facts.

I don't worry about the American Dream anymore. I have now defined my own dreams. I don't live in the future. I welcome today and make the best of it. If I am blessed to see tomorrow, then we will focus on tomorrow. I know first-hand that when you fail to prioritize and lose sight of what is really important, overload will surely follow.

# My Only Responsibility

Today, I have balance. However, it hasn't always been this way. There was a time when it appeared there just were not enough hours in the day. I possessed the perfect storm of responsibilities. Each day, I attempted to fulfill a multitude of roles perfectly. Let me give you some idea of what I mean.

***Wife.*** My husband is the chief of the Birmingham Fire Department in Birmingham, Alabama. He is responsible for 32 stations, approximately 760 personnel, and a city population of 250,000. His job requires him to be accessible 24 hours a day. It is not uncommon for the Fire Department to call in the wee hours (i.e., anytime after I have fallen asleep). It would be an understatement to say he has a very demanding job.

If you think we have equal responsibilities when it comes to the household and children, you would be dead wrong. I imagine that being the perfect wife would not be as challenging, but only if that were my only responsibility; but it is not.

***Mother.*** I am a mother of two very busy boys. Jae is nine, and Matthew is seven. They are typical little boys; always into something. They possess selective hearing. When I call for them to make up their beds or come do their homework, I can hear a pin drop. I say dinner is ready, and they run up the steps cheering.

Keeping up with their daily schedule and commitments at times is very challenging. However, I understand it is critical to a child's growth and development that the parents be fully engaged and involved. I imagine that accomplishing this task would not be as challenging if that were my only responsibility; but it is not.

***Career Woman.*** I work full-time. This year, I achieved 20 years with the same company. I started out as an engineer and have had the privilege of progressing through the ranks. A corporate environment is not for the faint of heart, especially if one aspires to move up. Sustaining a career over two decades with the same company would probably not seem as challenging if that were my only responsibility; but it is not.

***Servant.*** One would think wife, mother, and career woman would be enough, but I feel a strong urge—actually an obligation—to be actively involved in my church and community. Serving others and helping the community become a better place can be very time consuming, but it is also very rewarding. I imagine how many lives I could impact if that was my only responsibility; but it is not.

***Caregiver.*** When you are young, your parents provide for all your needs. They are there for you in the good times and bad. They kiss the boo-boos and clean up the messes large and small. They love you unconditionally. They guide and teach you life lessons to ensure you are ready to fly when you leave the nest.

Years passed, and the roles reversed. My parents are older and require more of my attention. With my father having Alzheimer's, it has added to the level of care they need. He and I live 300 miles apart, and it isn't possible to provide daily personal care. I do what I can. I know I would do more if this were my only responsibility; but it is not.

The roles seem endless, and so was my pursuit of perfection—unsuccessful, I might add. Have you heard the expression, "Jack-of-all-trades, master of none?" I was neither Jack nor master. I felt like I was always holding on to the handle of a train that was pulling out from the station at 200 miles per hour. I just could not gain solid footing.

On the outside, it appeared I had it all together. On the inside, all systems were on overload. The circumstances that existed were due to my inability to balance work and life. This was a clear case of self-inflicted overload.

Allowing work to dominate life and fearing failure added to the overwhelming pressure to hold it all together. I was in constant pursuit of that non-existent state of perfection. I was overwhelmed and overloaded, but it wasn't long before I found out what I thought was overwhelming was nothing compared to what I was about to face.

During this time, I had a good life, all things considered. I was married to a loving, caring, strong, godly man. I had two healthy, handsome, happy little boys. I lived in a nice house in a great neighborhood. My career was in decent shape. Overall, I would say I had a bright future ahead of me. I was at my prime.

Then in September 2008, everything changed. I was totally blindsided by the events that followed. This entire ordeal began with a routine annual checkup, which included a mammogram. The film showed a small mass. My doctor advised that it was probably nothing. To be sure, the doctor directed me to take a more intense mammogram. Once again, the mass showed up. Then I was directed to have a biopsy.

The day I was scheduled to hear the results, I went to the doctor's office by myself. My husband had agreed to go with me, but I told him that it wasn't necessary. That was a mistake. Sitting in that doctor's office waiting for the results from the biopsy felt like an eternity. All kinds of thoughts were going through my mind. How long do I have to live? Who's going to raise my children? Will my breast have to be removed? Why me? Why now? Am I being punished? This is not fair.

Then I had a bipolar moment.

My thoughts switched to dismissive mode. It isn't anything. Everything is fine. You are a woman of faith. You do not have to worry. What will I cook for dinner tonight? Then the door opened. The doctor sat down across from me, and she said the words I dreaded hearing: "You have breast cancer." In less than 10 seconds I felt every emotion imaginable: fear, anger, denial, worry, confusion, then back to fear. She was still talking to me about the diagnosis, but I had totally zoned out.

Once I regained awareness, there was some good news. The cancer was caught in Stage 1. The bad news was it was still cancer. I began radiation treatments immediately. In February 2009, I was declared cancer free.

Facing mortality caused me to reevaluate my priorities and look at life from a new perspective: Life will deliver its own set of natural problems. Why create more unnecessarily? Why stress over mess? Why pursue perfection when it is not humanly possible to achieve? Why lose sleep because of things you have no control over? Why pray if you are going to worry?

Admitting you have a problem is always the first step to recovery. Hello, my name is Joyce, and I HAD some problems. PEACE is what I have today. PEACE is an acronym for the five-step strategy I created and executed to achieve work-life balance and reduce the overload. We will explore each step shortly.

# Got PEACE?

Webster's Dictionary defines peace as a state of tranquility; freedom from disturbance. How much sweeter life would be if each day were filled with peace. Peace is the result of work and life being in balance.

All people are different and have different needs and desires. What motivates one person may not motivate another. Several things moved me to desire work-life balance. However, it takes more than desire. It also requires a willingness to implement a strategy. My husband, my children, and a longing to be whole are factors that motivated me to do better and be better. I was sick and tired of being sick and tired.

When I attended my son's program at school, I was sitting there thinking about everything I had to do back at the office. I felt so guilty not giving my undivided attention to my son. Then, when I was in the office, I found myself anxiously thinking about everything I had to do when I got home. Once home, there was homework to do, dinner to cook, a house to clean, and clothes to wash. At the end of the night, I had no desire for anyone or anything but sleep. There were times I was so tired at the end of the day, mentally and physically, that I just cried.

It was no one's fault but my own. I had successfully inflicted this overload on my life. I knew I had a problem when I would go to the master bathroom to find some "Me" time. I had magazines, my iPod, laptop, and, on occasion, snacks. When my family would come looking for me, I would say I was using the bathroom. It was partially true. I was using the bathroom as a safe room, because I was overloaded.

What I find amazing is I was very good at offering advice to my sisters or girl-friends. When they implemented my great ideas for work-life balance, I could clearly see they were doing better, feeling better, and living better. It was time for me to take my own advice.

If I was going to become all that I was created to be and desired to be, I had to get real, get motivated, and get up. Whether my motivation was purely for self or for the family, they both were worthy causes for me to not only talk about work-life balance, but to do something about it.

The way you know when something or someone is truly important to you is when you will sacrifice and commit to doing what it takes to be your very best. When you are in a rut, overloaded, and your "A game" looks more like your "D game," that is what you will offer. The best is what you offer when you are at your best.

At this point, I bring you to the crossroads. You are now at the intersection of self-inflicted overload and PEACE. Which road will you take? There is a more decisive question to answer: Got Peace? Whether your answer is yes or no, I invite you to read on and explore the five steps to work-life balance. This is an opportunity to begin conquering this work-life thing or enhance what you are already doing to maintain work-life balance.

Notes:

_____

_____

_____

_____

_____

_____

_____

_____

_____

_____

Notes:

_____
_____
_____
_____
_____
_____
_____
_____
_____
_____
_____

Notes:

_____

_____

_____

_____

_____

_____

_____

_____

_____

_____

_____

**Part II**

# PEACE

Pray

Energize

Adjust Your Attitude

Communicate

ENJOY

"The way you know when something or someone is truly important to you is when you will sacrifice and commit to doing what it takes to be your very best."

# Step 1: Pray
## Take It to the Altar

The first and most important step in achieving work-life balance is prayer. Prayer is the act of speaking with God. In very simple terms, prayer is communicating with the Father. Nothing formal is required. Just talk. He listens, and He responds. I am a firm believer in prayer. Prayer gives me straight, unobstructed access to my Father. With Him, I am free to express my praise, hopes, dreams, concerns, or anything on my mind.

From childhood, I was taught to say my prayers before I went to bed each night. I actually thought that I could deposit prayers to be used for the future. On one particular night, I forgot to say my prayers and jumped in bed. My Mother came to the door to say goodnight and asked if I had said my prayers. I said no and immediately climbed out of bed to correct my failure.

The next night when it was time to go to bed, I got on my knees and said my prayers. Unbeknownst to me, my mother was watching. She noticed that I prayed for an extended period of time. When I finished, I climbed into bed. Mother asked if everything was okay.

"Is something bothering you?" I said no.

Then she asked, "Why did you pray so long?"

I confidently replied, "I said the Lord's Prayer seven times." I figured that if I forgot to say my prayers one night that week, I would be covered.

I understand now that prayer is more than just an exercise. I have experienced enough unexpected events in my life that I have no doubt that prayer is extremely powerful. Do not be misled. One can pray all day, but if you don't have faith, you are wasting your time. Hebrews 11:1 explains that faith is "the substance of things hoped for, the evidence of things not seen." If I pray for work and life to be balanced, I must believe that God will answer my prayer.

Prayer is likened to water. It is a necessity for survival. You can go without water for a limited amount of time. However, without it, eventually you will die. The same is true with prayer and faith.

In times of difficulty, I fervently pray. I have an understanding and an unwavering trust in the Lord. As a result, I pray in all circumstances, good and bad, always finding comfort in knowing He is with me and I am not alone on this journey.

Family and friends may come and go. Situations will arise. In a time when nothing seems 100 percent except death and taxes, prayer brings me to a place where there is peace. I receive His unconditional love and grace consistently. There is no reason to fear when you have faith.

Prior to achieving work-life balance, I found myself dreading and, on occasion, resenting everything I had to do (i.e., work, cook, homework, etc). The blame game was becoming more frequent. Everyone was responsible for my dilemma. It was not my fault. I was a victim. Yeah, right!

I was a victim of my own self-inflicted overload. Prayer enables me to release that built-up frustration. Initially, my prayers were very selfish. Help me, me, me, and me. I have finally come to the realization it's not all about me. I now thank God for my circumstances. Through these circumstances, I have been blessed and have been a blessing to others.

There are countless stories in the Bible where "The effectual fervent prayer of a righteous man availeth much" (James 5:16(b)). Daniel in the lion's den; David and Goliath; Shadrach, Meshach, and Abednego; and Job are a few examples of prayers being answered. In each event, more than human will was needed to overcome the circumstances. The power of the Lord was the only source for victory over the adversity. If God delivered them, He could deliver me, too. I needed both victory and deliverance from my self-inflicted overload.

Prayer has brought me through some very tough times personally, professionally, financially, and spiritually. When my second son was born, he was diagnosed with a severe case of jaundice, and the prognosis was not good. I, along with family and friends, prayed for his deliverance from this condition. My prayers were answered. Matthew is 7 years old and totally healthy.

Prayer helped me stand up against cancer. I prayed for recovery. I prayed for acceptance. I prayed for my husband and sons. I prayed for peace. The more I prayed, the closer I felt to God. The closer I felt to God, the more peace I gained about this entire situation. Through this experience, I learned what the saying, "I have a peace that surpasses all understanding," means.

Prayer is helping me cope with aging parents, particularly my Dad, who was diagnosed with Alzheimer's in 2010. To say it is hard to watch someone you love slowly fade away would be an understatement. If it wasn't for prayer, I would feel totally helpless. Prayer gives me the assurance that everything is going to be fine.

Prayer has helped me put things in perspective. Have you ever had an issue that would just not go away? It kept you up at night. It affected your perspective on life. It altered your mood for the worse every time the issue was brought up. I've been there. Not having peace about something definitely affects how balanced your world will be.

Through prayer, I was able to gain understanding and strength to release the hurts and pains that I believed my Dad caused my family. I no longer feel the need to judge, nor do I hold anything against him. I can actually give him honor. Bad, good, or indifferent, he is my Daddy. He loves me in his own way, and I do love him. In the past, I would say, "I am who I am in spite of my Dad." Now, I know I am who I am *because* of my Dad.

I can recall another situation where I had lost sight of where blessings come from. I was ordering my own steps. Mistake. The more I focused on the career, the less I focused on family and became extremely frustrated. I was in a very dark place. Work-life balance was so out of whack that it affected everyone around me, as well as myself.

When my husband could not take any more of my attitude, he reminded me that God had already blessed me; and until I became thankful for what I had, I would continue to block my blessings (i.e., promotion). This was a major turning point to achieving work-life balance.

I returned to the altar with a new perspective and a new prayer, the Serenity Prayer. "God grant me the serenity to accept the things I cannot change, courage to change the things I can, and the wisdom to know the difference."

Cancer, my son, my Dad, career, and many other circumstances were all taken to the Father in prayer. I have no doubt that I have come through them all better, stronger, and liberated because my prayers were answered.

Whatever is going on that causes your world to be unbalanced, I encourage you to take the first step and pray. My daily prayer is, "Lord, lead me in the way You would have me to go. Help me to be a blessing to someone, and shower me with Your favor."

To achieve work-life balance, you may find you need to let some stuff go. Unresolved issues are heavy burdens to carry. I highly recommend you take those burdens to the altar and lay them down. Let go, and let God.

# *Step 2: Energize*

## Making It Through the Day

To be in the very best possible condition to meet one's obligation, I recommend Step 2: Energize. Running on adrenaline can only last for so long before something falls through the cracks or worse. You may be the one that falls through the cracks.

When you have a laundry list of responsibilities, where do you get the energy to endure? Do you find yourself eating fast food on the go? Is getting a minimum of eight hours sleep each night foreign to you? Have you neglected to take care of your body, your mind, and your soul?

I would bet you answered yes to at least one of these questions. There was a time I would have answered yes, as well. Not that I did not care about myself. I just found myself caring more for others. Honorable? Yes. Wise? No.

It is a rewarding feeling to help and care for someone, particularly someone you love. It is rewarding to know that you are making a difference in the lives of others. Actually, we are called to help others. However, if over time that assistance causes you discomfort and imbalance, you need a strategy.

You must take care of self, so you can effectively take care of those you love. Think of it like this: When traveling by air, the flight attendant recites the emergency safety instructions. Do you recall hearing them say, "If the cabin loses pressure, place the oxygen mask on yourself first, and then place it on the child?"

The same principle applies to anyone who wants to achieve work-life balance. Before you can effectively take care of everyone else, the first order of business is to effectively take care of you. This includes care for your body, mind, and soul.

## Body

There are numerous methods to care for the body, mind, and soul. My strategy to energize the body is to exercise at least three times a week for 45 minutes. My beverage of choice is water. I do not smoke, nor do I drink anymore. I make every effort to get seven to eight hours of sleep each night. I also limit my intake of fast food.

I continue to seek ways to improve my physical health. There are several people very close to me who suffer from a variety of physical ailments. The causes of the ailments range from age and heredity to habits and priorities. Some of the best lessons we can learn are the ones that are right in front of our eyes. There are consequences to your actions and inaction. The right thing to do is to recognize them and do something about them.

Do you want to be out of breath after walking up a flight of steps? Do you want to be on medication for hypertension, diabetes, or cholesterol? Do you want to experience aches and pains? Much of this can be avoided if you take the time to take care of your physical health. In the long run, it will help you live longer, healthier, and with more energy.

## Mind

The mind plays a key part in maintaining work-life balance. The mind is not able to operate at peak capacity if you are sleep-deprived or wrought with worry. I said it earlier—losing sleep does not change the circumstances. Go to sleep. Rest your mind. Tackle the world tomorrow.

When I was in an overloaded state of mind, I made questionable decisions. Decisions made during these times seemed reasonable. Later, when I was in a better state of mind, I had second thoughts and regrets. This could have been avoided if I had been patient and rested, particularly when it came to responding to my children's requests or performing relatively simple tasks.

For example: How smart was it for me to tell my 5-year-old that he can put the bubble bath in the bathtub? Mistake. I did not think that through. You know what happened. He poured half the bottle in the tub. The result was mounds of bubbles and a mess to clean up.

Overload can also cause hurt feelings. I would never intentionally hurt someone's feelings. However, speaking without thinking can get you in a lot of trouble. I was visiting a friend who had just purchased his first home. He was so excited and proud of this accomplishment. I was also happy for him. On this day, he insisted that I see the new house. Against my best judgment, I accepted the invitation. I was tired and really did not have the time to drop by, due to a list of other commitments I had. In hindsight, I should have taken a rain check.

I arrived and tried to quickly tour the home. The happy tour was moving in slow motion. Then came the question, "What do you think of my new home?" Without thinking, I quickly said, "This is a cute little house." I knew immediately by his expression I said the wrong thing. This home was a major accomplishment. It was like a mansion to someone who had always rented a small apartment. I undervalued him and his home. To say I put my foot in my mouth would be an understatement. If I had been in a balanced state, this very awkward situation could have been avoided. Instead, I successfully damaged a friendship. I was just not thinking. We made peace eventually, but it took some time.

The saying goes, "The mind is a terrible thing to waste." I agree. The mind is also a terrible thing to overload. If the mind is energized, you have a better opportunity to make the best decisions for you and those who depend upon you. Take time, clear your mind, and exhale.

### Soul

I define soul as the spiritual part of a person's being that monitors one's moral and emotional feeling. I energize my soul by making positive deposits. Scripture, laughter, music, chocolate, and spa days are a few examples of deposits. The soul is like a bank account—the more deposits you make, the more dividends the account will pay. I am better equipped to handle adversity, pressures, or overload when my spiritual account is full.

The second step in achieving work-life balance is not about having the energy to manage the overload. It is about having the physical, mental, and spiritual strength to avoid the overload before it arises. How and what you do to maintain your energy is up to you.

# *There should be no guilt*

# *in taking care of self.*

*It is commendable to give and help others. However, you must be at your best to give the very best.*

**Ways to Energize Your Body, Mind, and Soul**

**TIP:**

o **Go to bed early** – By 10 p.m., if possible.

o **Eat healthy snacks** – Prepare and carry snacks with you.

o **Surround yourself with positive people** – Birds of the same feather flock together.

o **Make time for self** – Relax, rejuvenate, unwind.

o **Expand your knowledge** – Learn a new language, join a community theater.

o **Volunteer** – It is better to give than receive.

# Step 3: Adjust Your Attitude

## Get Over It

The third step in achieving work-life balance is having the right attitude. Attitude is all about perspective. It is one's response, behavior, or emotion toward how you see the world. "Is your glass half empty or half full?" I would challenge you to say, "It doesn't matter if your glass is half empty or half full. Just be thankful you have a glass." It is this kind of attitude that contributes greatly to achieving work-life balance.

There are many things we cannot control. We cannot control the weather, stock market, time of death, time of birth, who likes us, or who dislikes us. What you *can* control is your attitude. Your attitude can turn what appears to be the worst circumstance into one that is the ultimate, awesome, best.

Let's look at something as simple as the morning drive to work. Traffic is slow. It is bumper to bumper. There are on-looker delays. It is pretty clear, unless you have lights and sirens, you are going to be late for work.

A person with a negative attitude would spend time whining, complaining, blowing the horn, and possibly tailgating. Sounds like a clear case of morning road rage. This attitude causes the blood pressure to go up, increases stress levels, and becomes a potential set-up for an accident. This attitude does not get you to work any faster.

Now, let's explore the same scenario with a positive attitude. I accept that traffic is bad, and I will more than likely be late for work. I call the office and inform the boss of my delay. He says, "I heard about a bad accident on Interstate 65 and the traffic backup. Take your time, and be safe. See you when you arrive." That is handled. Let's make the best of this time. Several ideas occur: call Mom and check on the family, listen to my favorite morning talk show, or just chill and meditate. All three options are much more beneficial than being a morning road warrior.

Yes, I could have left earlier, but I didn't. Get over it. The key is to look at every situation as how you can make the best of it now that you are in it.

When I was diagnosed with breast cancer, my attitude oscillated between positive and negative. One minute I was angry and questioning God, then the next I was ready to fight for my life. I was a mess.

Then something happened that caused me to adjust my entire attitude. I went each morning prior to work for radiation treatments. On this particular morning, I was dressed to the nines, hair and nails were perfect, and even the car was clean. I was really cute that morning, and I was feeling good. I had a very positive attitude.

When I walked in the changing lounge, several ladies were sitting there waiting to have their treatments, and the atmosphere was quite depressing. There was a feeling of sadness and despair in the air. Not for long. I immediately took it upon myself to cheer the ladies up. As we talked and shared our diagnoses, one lady said I did not look like I have cancer. I told her that was the plan. I was not going to allow my attitude to cause me to surrender to cancer. Cancer was not going to control me. From that day until the end of my treatments, the ladies were waiting to see what I was wearing each day, and I looked forward to seeing them and lighting up the room with my positive attitude.

Life offers everyone challenges, adversities, and disappointments. How you handle them is what sets the winners apart from the losers. Attitudes can also be contagious. There was just as much opportunity for me to become depressed when I walked in the cancer treatment center as it was for everyone to cheer up when I arrived.

Attitude is about choices. How you choose to respond has a direct effect on work-life balance. Having a bad attitude about the circumstances just makes matters worst. In the big scheme of life, what causes a bad attitude is often really minute. I have met individuals who are facing some of the greatest challenges in life (e.g., multiple sclerosis, autism, double mastectomy, unemployment, divorce, and the list goes on). Each one of these individuals was living with a positive attitude. They find all that is good in their situation. What is more amazing is they all tend to help and uplift others.

How much more balanced one would be if we could only see the positive in everything. How often do we have a bad attitude or pessimistic perspective on things that are not life-threatening? Have you ever been in the grocery store line with less than 10 items, and the person in front of you has an overflowing buggy? I bet you wished they would offer to let you go first, but they don't. What kind of attitude do you have? Are you sulking and thinking bad things about the person in front of you? Or do you see this as an opportunity to pick up a magazine at the register and catch up on the latest entertainment news?

It is inevitable that the unexpected will occur. How you respond is all about your attitude. I do not always immediately respond to what life dishes out with a positive attitude. However, the time delay between attitude adjustments has become much shorter.

The simplest occurrences can change the daily balance when the wrong attitude exists. It has been said, "Don't sweat the small stuff." If it isn't a life-and-death occurrence, isn't it all small stuff? No time to cook, being looked over for a promotion, and an unclean house are a few examples of small issues I would sweat over, thus affecting my balance. With a new perspective and a better attitude, look what can happen. No time to cook dinner? Order pizza. Looked over for a promotion? Trust that God has something better for you. House isn't clean? Time to delegate.

*There is good in everything. You must have the right attitude and choose to see it.*

# *Step 4: Communicate*

## Commit, Delay, or Shut It Down

Communication is the exchange of information, thought, and/or opinion. Simply stated, communication is talking and listening. While in college, I made a conscious decision to communicate with my professor when I was in a difficult situation. The outcome of this decision has led me to include communication in my strategy to achieve work-life balance.

After taking the final exam for my physics course, I left and went to the park to have a pity party. I knew it was over for me. The thought of not passing a class was devastating, particularly since I had never made a grade lower than a C. After sitting there for a while, I thought if I could convince the instructor to give me an incomplete grade, I could take the class again.

I went back and talked with the instructor. What happened was remarkable. I got more than I hoped for. The instructor apologized to me. He said if a student came to every class, every study session, and still did not understand the material, he failed to do his job. He offered the following: If I agreed to take Physics II from him the next semester, he would give me a C. How many teachers today would take responsibility for a student not passing a class because of their failure to teach? As a result of just communicating, we both received a second chance.

## Methods for Successful Communication

**TIP:**

○ **Saying no to avoid over-committing**

○ **Listening and learning from the wisdom of others**

○ **Asking for help when necessary**

A failure to communicate can cause overload. How many times have you been asked for a "small favor" that turns into more than you expected?

Example: "Would you pick my child up from school? I'll be there as soon as I get off work."

"No problem," you say. "I'll be happy to."

After work doesn't mean 5:30 p.m., as you assumed, though. After work actually means 9-ish, possibly 10:00. What was just a pickup from school now includes feeding, homework, and postponing of whatever you had planned.

Now rewind.

"Would you pick my child up from school? I'll be there as soon as I get off work."

"What time do you get off work?"

She responds, "9 p.m."

Ball is in your court. After giving it some thought, you have three choices: commit, delay, or shut it down.

# Saying No

*Commit* and accept everything that goes with it. Be mindful of your responsibilities, tasks, and attitude. Once you commit, this is now your responsibility, and you should feel no regrets.

*Delay* results in excuses why you can't do it. Delay leaves you open for your mind to be changed, particularly if the excuse is weak. It has been said that an excuse is just a dressed-up lie. The truth will set you free.

*Shut it down* releases you from the possibility of overload. When you are trying to achieve work-life balance, it is in your best interest to shut the request down. I admit it. I could not say no. I never wanted to disappoint anyone. Now, I realize those who really care will understand when I say no. It gets easier. You should try it. Say it. No, No, No, No!

> **TIP:**
>
> **If you find it difficult or impolite to just say no, here is an alternative response to shut it down.**
>
> 1. **Express Appreciation**
> 2. **Acknowledge Request**
> 3. **Tell the Truth**
>
> **Example:**
>
> *"Thank you for entrusting me to pick your child up from school. I would love to help you, but I am unavailable at this time."*

This method offers the same result as saying No. You shut it down and have successfully avoided self- inflicted overload.

Exception and sacrifice should always be considered. We are called to help one another. However, you should do it for the right reasons. If you do, there will be no complaining or regrets after you commit. If it really isn't feasible to fill the favor, just be honest, communicate, and shut it down.

## Listen and Learn

Be willing to listen to the wisdom and advice of those who have traveled the road you are embarking upon. I bet there is someone in your life—mother, teacher, friend, or co-worker—who has or will share his or her experience with you. They will tell you about lessons learned, mistakes made. I encourage you to listen. No reason to reinvent the wheel.

As I said earlier, my mom and sometimes my four older sisters have offered both solicited and unsolicited advice that has been very helpful. I get advice ranging from recipes to raising children. The things I learn help me to better navigate the ups and downs of daily living, thus contributing to that ultimate state of PEACE.

## Ask for Help

There was a time I would not ask for help. To me, asking for help represented weakness or failure. This behavior resulted in a severe case of self-inflicted overload. I was running from commitment to commitment, eating on the go, and feeling overwhelmed. Everything was rush, rush, and rush. I tried to do too much with too little—too little time, too little help, and too little patience.

Performing simple tasks became somewhat difficult. Something as routine as preparing a meal or putting together an outfit became challenging. Feeling overloaded became the norm, but not anymore. I begin each day by making a daily to-do list. Then I quickly prioritize what has to be done. I've found that some tasks may be postponed, removed, or may require seeking some help. There is no shame in asking for advice or help. The ultimate goal is to not become overwhelmed or overloaded. If asking for help achieves that end, go for it.

My husband is the first person I seek help from. We work together so we can both experience balance. Throughout the day, we constantly communicate, touch base, and collectively manage some of the duties of the day (i.e., children, dinner, meetings, etc). I do not wish to mislead you. It still isn't 50/50, but I can accept 60/40.

Be warned. All help is not free. If a clean house contributes to that feeling of peace, hire a cleaning service. If having a balanced, home-cooked meal contributes to that feeling of peace, order takeout from a restaurant that offers healthy meals. If you need some "me time" and don't know what to do with the kids or a pet, consider finding a certified day camp or kennel. Invest in whatever it takes to achieve work-life balance. It will pay dividends.

Establishing a support system or network is another source of assistance. Communicating is key to establishing a network. A network can be defined as a group of people who communicate with one another and work together as a unit to achieve a common end. There are all kinds of networks. Establishing a network that assists in managing your daily duties can be very effective.

There are advantages to having a network. How so? Consider the following: You are in desperate need of a service, advice, or information. Do you really want to gamble on researching your need in the yellow pages? It would be better to know someone who knows someone. Having a trusted network enables you the flexibility to make contacts, receive referrals, and secure the service you need in a more timely and efficient manner.

It is important to establish mutually beneficial relationships before you need them. One network I have benefitted from is made up of firefighters. Many firefighters have second careers. Since my husband is a firefighter, he has many relationships in the fire service. Every time we needed home repairs and renovations, there were always firefighters in the network who could provide the service or give a trusted referral. I also have a child care network and career network. It is such a relief when you have more than one person to call upon when you are in need of something.

People cannot read your mind. Express yourself. Saying no, listening to advice, and/or asking for help are small steps toward work-life balance and a big step toward eliminating self-inflicted overload.

# Step 5: Enjoy

## This Is the Day

Like many people, I am guilty of taking life for granted. I have procrastinated. I have delayed. I have made excuses. All for a false belief that tomorrow will come. Maybe it will. Then again, maybe it won't. I have never seen a daily newspaper that listed no one on the obituaries page. A day doesn't pass that someone doesn't expire. Let's accept the facts: Once it is over, it is over. Each morning when you wake up, you are given the gift of life. That alone should bring you joy. There are limitless possibilities with the birth of a new day.

As I prioritize my day, I am always mindful to leave some time for simple pleasures that bring me joy. That joy can be as simple as working on a painting after everyone has gone to bed, taking the boys for a slushy after school, or meeting my husband for lunch, or as elaborate as taking a day of vacation to go get a massage.

Joy is an emotion that is generated by your internal outlook on the external world. It has been said that happiness is dependent upon what is happening. We cannot always control what happens; therefore, being happy isn't guaranteed. Joy is dependent upon you.

I recall being in labor with my first child. Do you really think any woman can be happy when she has 7 lbs., 11 ounces trying to exit a very small doorway? The realization that a miracle is about to arrive is nothing but joy. The memory of almost failing physics in college doesn't bring happiness. As I look back on the experience, I now have joy and peace.

I am fully aware that tomorrow is not promised. Therefore, I make every effort to balance each day. Note that I did not say every day. Each day means one day. Every day refers to multiple days. Yes, we should have long-range plans. However, we cannot neglect today. I focus on balancing each day as it comes. Tomorrow is not here. Yesterday is gone. You have today. Choose to enjoy it.

When work and life are out of balance, it is more difficult to be joyful. Enjoyment is the farthest thing from your mind, because you are inundated with tasks and responsibilities. However, it is imperative for the PEACE strategy to be successful—you must enjoy each day.

Imagine what you would do if you knew today would be your last day to live. Would you wish you could go back and do some things differently? Were there some fences you needed to mend? Did you take that vacation you always wanted to take? Have you kept all your promises you made? Did you help someone along the way?

Let there be no misunderstanding. Life without joy isn't much of a life. How sad it would be to look back over your life and find that you did not live life to the fullest. You only existed.

Another aspect of having joy is not living with regrets. I learned a very important lesson about regrets the hard way. I missed the opportunity to do what was in my heart for reasons that now seem very selfish and so trivial.

I had a great deal of respect and love for my college friend's grandfather. His grandfather, who we called "Tops," was a small man with a very big presence. He had such a calming confidence. He was a godly man. I enjoyed going into the garage when he was working and listening to his stories and advice.

When Tops became terminally ill, he was brought home from the hospital. Medically, there was nothing more that could be done. His time was drawing to a close. I would go to the house but would not go in his bedroom to see him. I just did not want to see him in that state.

It was a Friday evening when I asked my friend how his grandfather was doing, and he said, "Not well." I told him I would go see his grandfather the next day. It was a few hours later, and we received the call that Tops had died. I missed the opportunity to tell Tops how much I loved him and thank him for always being there. The opportunity is eternally gone.

Yes, he knew it, but I regret not telling him. I assumed I had time. I was so wrong, and I regretted it for a long time. With every regret comes a lesson. Since that time, I have never made that same mistake.

My grandmother had a saying: "Give me my flowers now." I am purposeful in giving flowers while I have a chance. Flowers can be actual flowers, a note, a "thinking about you" call, or a smile to a passing stranger. Whatever it is, give it now. Bring some joy to someone today, and in turn, you will receive joy.

## *This is the day that the Lord has made. Let us rejoice and be glad in it.*

This passage of scripture now means so much to me.

Notes:

_____

_____

_____

_____

_____

_____

_____

_____

_____

_____

_____

Notes:

_____
_____
_____
_____
_____
_____
_____
_____
_____
_____
_____

Notes:

_____

_____

_____

_____

_____

_____

_____

_____

_____

_____

_____

**Part III**

# On Your Mark, Get Set, Choose

"When you choose to balance work and life and eliminate self-inflicted overload, you can have, become, and achieve just about anything."

# On Your Mark. Get Set. Choose!

What's stopping you from achieving work-life balance?  What causes you to experience overload?  Are you at your very best?  The answer to these questions boils down to one word: Choice.

From a very early age we begin to make choices. As a child, choosing a toy to play with is the first of many choices made in a person's lifetime.  As time passes, we grow and start to make more critical choices about our lives.

We choose to marry, stay single or settle. We choose to have children, adopt, or not.  We choose to challenge, accept, or ignore the status quo. We choose to live life to the fullest or just exist.  There are countless choices we have the power to make.

Earlier on, I made choices that were not necessarily in my best interest.  Peer pressure and indecisive behavior resulted in choices that I am not proud of.  However, there is a bright side to those choices.  I learned valuable lessons and can now say first-hand what deliverance really is.

I was once single with no children, a great job, and the freedom to make choices that affected no one but me.  That is not the case now.  I am married with children and recognize the world doesn't evolve around me.  The choices I make have a direct impact on not only me, but also my family.

My family is the main reason I chose to develop a strategy to achieve work-life balance.  They are my motivation.  It is my desire to give my very best.  Therefore,

I make choices to help me become my very best. Choosing to be balanced rather than overloaded directly contributes to becoming your best.

The strategy I offer to you is intended to help you achieve work-life balance. I welcome you to test it out in its entirety or choose whichever elements will work for you. The beauty of a strategy is it can evolve. Depending on your circumstances, you may only need prayer and communication. Your circumstances may dictate a totally different strategy.

Incorporating prayer, energy, adjusting your attitude, communication, and enjoyment in my daily life has had an enormous effect on my psyche, relationships, health, and my expectations for the future. Achieving work-life balance has empowered me to be confident in the choices I make. It has made me a better wife, mother, friend, employee, and advocate.

Today, I choose to profess my faith and beliefs without regard to judgment. I choose to make self a priority. I choose to see the world through rose-colored glasses. I choose to seek the wisdom of others. I choose to celebrate this day. I choose to be me without any apologies.

We all have the privilege to choose. Some choices we make are intentional. Some choices made may be by accident. Then, there is the choice to do nothing. Although you may choose to do nothing, that is still a choice you have made.

With every choice made intentionally or unintentionally, there are consequences. The strategy I have chosen to live by lends itself to a peaceful consequence. My heart goes out to those who, for whatever reason, seem to continue to live an imbalanced life. The longer the imbalance exists, the longer the risk for negative consequences will last.

Who wants to live life stressed, overwhelmed, unhappy, fearful, tired, and unhealthy? All these conditions can occur without balance. To choose to do nothing or do the same things over and over will result in the same outcome. "If you always do what you have always done, you will always get what you always got."

Are you ready to choose a strategy? I encourage you to choose the PEACE strategy. It won't cost you a dime to pray. Taking care of your mind, body, and soul cannot be optional. It is an absolute necessity for survival. A positive attitude will attract positive consequences.

Speak up and listen up. Choose to effectively communicate. There is no shame in asking for help or seeking the wisdom of others.

Last but not least, choose to enjoy the life you have. Who you are and where you are at this time is not by accident. It is easy to think that the life someone else is living is more appealing or better than yours. Do not be misled. The grass you think is greener on the other side of the fence may actually be artificial turf.

When you choose to balance work and life and eliminate self-inflicted overload, you can have, become, and achieve just about anything. I believe the only limits that exist are the ones we place upon ourselves. Consider marathon runners. These individuals have to possess a great deal of discipline and determination to achieve such a feat. The term "hitting the wall" refers to a runner who has hit their limit. To overcome this wall, runners push past the mental and physical discomfort one step at a time until they reach the finish line. The marathon runner has chosen to believe there are no limits.

The same is true for us. We can choose to hit the wall and be limited, or we can choose to push through, and the potential results are limitless.

Be encouraged. Yesterday is gone. Tomorrow is not here. Today is what we have at this moment in time. Choose the very best that life has to offer while you are here upon this great, beautiful earth. It is your choice. Remember, it is not over until you are six feet under.

Notes:

_____
_____
_____
_____
_____
_____
_____
_____
_____
_____
_____

Notes:

_____

_____

_____

_____

_____

_____

_____

_____

_____

_____

Notes:

_____
_____
_____
_____
_____
_____
_____
_____
_____
_____
_____

# Helpful Hints
## for
## Work-Life Balance

Servant

MOTHER

Driver | 1st Lady

Cook | Career Woman

Wife | Coach

Maid | Sister

Playmate | Advocate | Tutor

1. **Smile**
2. **Have faith.**
3. **Prioritize.**
4. **Listen and learn.**
5. **Avoid overload.**
6. **Focus on today.**
7. **Show gratitude.**
8. **Help someone.**
9. **Make positive choices.**
10. **Check your attitude.**
11. **Care for body, mind, and soul.**
12. **Stop and smell the flowers.**
13. **Don't sweat the small stuff.**
14. **Love your neighbor as yourself.**
15. **Inspire others to live life to the fullest.**
16. **Envision the best that life has to offer.**
17. **Enjoy each day as if it were your last.**
18. **Celebrate the big and little successes.**
19. **Accept responsibility for your circumstances.**

Notes:

# Notes:

_____

_____

_____

_____

_____

_____

_____

_____

_____

_____

_____

Notes:

_____

_____

_____

_____

_____

_____

_____

_____

_____

_____

# Self-Inflicted Overload PEACE Contract

I, _____, am a very special individual. I desire and deserve to experience a life filled with PEACE.

I acknowledge I suffer from Self-Inflicted Overload. I accept full responsibility for the choices I have made or not made that have contributed to my condition.

I believe I can achieve anything I put my mind to. Therefore starting today, _____, I commit to making choices that will result in me experiencing a life filled with PEACE. I WILL become my very best.

I promise I will pray, energize my body, mind and soul, adjust my attitude and enjoy each day that I am given to live upon this earth.

This promise I make to myself.

Signature_____Date_____

Witness_____Date_____

# Acknowledgements

Thank you and much love to my mother, who instilled in me that the only limitations that exist in life are the ones I place upon myself. For most of my life, I thought I became the person I am in spite of my Father, but now, I know I am who I am because of him. Love you, Daddy.

To my husband and my best friend, all I can say is, "What did I do to deserve a man as loving as you?" Thank you for supporting me. I love you with all my heart.

Marsha Morgan, who extended the invitation for me to speak at Belle Inc. of Birmingham Celebration of Womanhood Summit. Thank you, Marsha. The feedback following that 25-minute talk on work-life balance inspired me to share my strategies with other women.

Ted Debro, my faithful church member who encouraged me to write a book long before I considered it. Thank you for sharing your prophecy and promising to purchase my first book.

To the reader: I sincerely thank you for giving me an opportunity to share my five-step strategy for achieving work-life balance. I hope this book has equipped you with information that assists you on your life's journey. May your journey be filled with **PEACE.**

# Biographical Sketch

Joyce E. Brooks holds a Bachelor of Science degree in electrical engineering from the University of South Alabama and a Master's degree in electrical engineering from the University of Alabama at Birmingham.

She was born and raised in Prichard, Alabama, by her parents, Eddie Vaughn and Hattie Lee Pettway. The youngest of seven children, the "baby of the bunch" moved to Birmingham, Alabama in 1991 to begin her career with Alabama Power.

In addition, Joyce is the wife of Birmingham Fire Chief Ivor J. Brooks, the mother of two very busy boys, two adult daughters and one granddaughter. She is an aspiring artist and playwright, as well as, a breast cancer survivor. She is also actively involved in her church and the community. Joyce proudly wears many hats. To say she is busy would be an understatement.

After being diagnosed with stage one breast cancer in September 2008, then being declared cancer free in 2009, Joyce stepped back and made a commitment to become her very best. Unfortunately, her very best was being hindered by her overloaded schedule and lack of work-life balance.

Joyce was an expert when it came to being overloaded, but not anymore. She stepped out on faith and pressed the reset button on her life. She walked away from a six-figure salary after 21 years with the same company. She became a full-time mom, something she had always desired to do, but put off. And she enjoys a new daily routine that includes exploring her creative side and helping others become their very best.

She is now an expert on how to eliminate the overload, achieve work-life balance, and gain that peace we all deserve. As the author of Self-Inflicted Overload, Joyce opens up about her personal journey to achieving peace and shares her five-step strategy to help others do the same.

For additional information, please visit: www.selfinflictedoverload.com